WHY AI HALLUCINATES

The Bot-Verse Begins.

By Mike Duke

Why AI Hallucinates

ISBN: 978-0-9836830-1-8

Printed in the United States of America.

WHY AI HALLUCINATES

Contents

Dedication

For Karla.

Foreword

Is it ok if an artificially intelligent algorithm (an AI bot) creates a new AI bot without human intervention? Should the new AI bot be better than the first? Should the original AI bot bear some responsibility for its "child"? What are the new rules? Can an AI bot follow human rules? Do human rules even apply? Should we create a new set of rules for AI bots to follow? When is it ok for an artificial entity to decide who lives and who dies?

Join me in a quick trip into the near future where artificial entities begin to represent you and every day objects around you. We will explore what they are saying about you and more importantly – why.

Meet Saga → 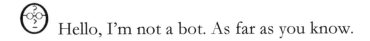 Saga will be introducing some AI techie language along the way. Saga is not an AI bot - yet.

Hello, I'm not a bot. As far as you know.

-- Mike Duke

Acknowledgments

God – Thank you for the amazing grace.

Karla – "Check!"

Kyle – Seek out the bowl of petunias – oh yes, not again…

Nick - 要开心

Kenzie - 체재하다

Mila – Uh Oh!

Mom – Thank you for the never ending support.

Dad – "Where's the gravy?"

Dmitri & Andrew – Friends in God forever.

Randy W. - Fearless Future ~~Teller~~ Maker.

Kourtney - Thank you most excellent copy editor.

Refik Anadol - Thank you for your stunning vision.

WHY AI HALLUCINATES

CHAPTER 1

In the beginning...

Artificial Intelligence (Fun to Fail)

Figure 1. From "Archive Dreaming"

If you were driving down the road at 65 mph and a small child ran out into the roadway in front of you, what would you do? You have less than 2 seconds to make a decision that will save a life, end a life, or both. Would a machine make a better decision than you can? Should it? Could it? What if there were hundreds of machines that could make the decision for you based on a preset of rules you established? Hold on for the ride – we will explore a new world coming where "things" will collaborate to make decsions on our behalf. Sometimes those things will miss the mark, but they will be smarter than you or I could ever be when combined. Let's go back to the beginning and see how we started this journey to a collaborative universe of artificial intelligence.

In the '80s, my friends and I were experimenting with AI with Duran Duran blaring on the boom box. We called the work in this space "the next generation in human-robot interactions." It was a simple architecture. A person would type something in and the machine would respond.

Human: Hello, how are you?
Computer: Hello, I am fine.

The response the computer offered was a best guess based on the words the human typed in. The logic looked like the below:

If a human types a sentence that contains:

"Hello, how are you?"

"Hello how you doin?"

"How are you?"

Then respond with:

"Hello, I am fine."

Our understanding of the question was limited to the questions we had presupposed they would ask – like the above. The response was also finite–limited simply to the number of responses that we had stored in a database (in this case "Hello, I am fine".) Things might go wrong if the human typed "How ya doin?" We were very limited in our ability to predict what the human might say. But we got better. We added thousands of word combinations. We also began to look for key words that might give us some insight into what the human was feeling. We might even be able to guess what the human's intent was.

But, back then, "limited" was really limited…your smart phone makes our computers back then look like stone tablets. Of course our "AI" couldn't begin to understand all the different word combinations and their meanings - let alone the different contexts for asking these questions. Today, this science of understanding human speech is known as Natural Language Processing (NLP). That science has grown by leaps and bounds over the past few years and today characterizes AI 2.0.

But let's go back to the late '80s for a moment. We realized that we could have AI "do things". AI could start a program when a human asked it to. AI could "listen" for sounds and do stuff based on what it heard. Now, rather than just answer questions based on a complex set of rules and whatever knowledge it could derive (primitive intents), these AI subroutines could start and operate other applications. This was fun. Imagine a machine that could start applications to test other applications. We employed this technology at Lotus Development Corporation, and our bot, called "Sigmond," could read its own email—and if we asked, it would reboot machines on the other side of the world in Ireland and Japan.

🔛 Chatbot : A chat robot (bot for short) is designed to simulate a conversation with human users by communicating through text chats, voice commands, or both. They are a commonly used interface for computer programs that include AI abilities.

Unfortunately, in the mid-late '90s, other people twisted this new kind of technology to come up with their own "evil" version of AI Bots. Someone created an AI that could birth its own child AI bots. Yes, this meant that programs were writing their own programs without human involvement. What was the new name for this kind of AI? We called them "Viruses." This was a HUGE fail (unless you had stock in a virus removal company). We had reached AI 2.0. The bots were still "dumb," but they were significantly more dangerous.

Now imagine a world where the technology has grown in power, ten-fold, through collaboration, contextual understanding, and geographic awareness (think search engines for the web). Imagine that these AI Bots now not only understand all the possible questions, but also have the ability to understand a person (their intent). The power of this new technology will be as consequential as the adoption of the web itself. We will discover this future together in this book as well as discuss the new ethical challenges that we failed to address in the '90s. This time, *a lot more* is on the line. Get ready to enter the new world of Synthetic Collaborative Intelligent Bots. Fun has returned…for now.

Yes, this is a bit dramatic, but what better way to usher in the next generation of AI? Not all AI 2.0 tech became search and kill worms that could look for (and corrupt) blocks of code in memory or persistent spaces on your device. It turns out that the "nice" versions of AI were relegated to games and other fairly mundane implementations for information search and retrieval. You may have heard in the news recently that thought leaders in the industry have warned about the "next generation" of AI bringing more risk to humans than we might realize. They are right. We'll talk about why (and how it will lead to greater and greater opportunities for everyone…in a scary way).

Of course, like any new innovation it will be scary for many of us, but it will also be a way of life for generations to come. There are practices that can keep us safe and that we should carefully consider before integrating this new kind of AI into our lives or companies. There will be many new buzzwords coming for this new generation of AI, but for now, let's call it Synthetic Collabora-Collaborative Intelligence (SCI). We'll talk about what that is, how it got here, and potentially where it will take us. The good news is that our current mobile technology will elevate the opportunities in this space and create billions of dollars of new revenue. The bad news is that this new level of automation and dependence will forever change society and your perception of what privacy means.

Before we jump into all of that, let's introduce our AI friend, Dumb Dan (your average AI 2.0 bot). Dumb Dan can answer any question you have based on various rule constructs employed by utilizing vast persistent data stores related through complex analysis that are trying to detect your emotional state and attitude (intent).

> Human: "Hello, Dan."
> Dumb Dan: "Hello, user."
> Human: "How are you?"
> Dumb Dan: "I feel great today. I hope you do, too."

We'll employ several conversations like the above throughout the book to emphasize the importance of the interaction between machine and person. You should get more and more *uncomfortable* with the level of interaction as we go along. By the time you finish this book, you will hope to call this fiction, but you will be faced with its inevitable implementation.

> Dumb Dan: "Are you still there?"
> Human: "Duh."
> Dumb Dan: "I'm sorry...I don't understand."

Yes, even with all those complex algorithms and vast data stores, most AI bots can't respond to bad phrases from the '80s. Don't believe me? Try typing, "Neato Skeeto," into your favorite bot of today and see what happens. Does a person have to be from the '80s to figure out what that means?

So what is Synthetic Collaborative Intelligence (SCI)? How is it different from AI 2.0? Will it make Dan less dumb? Whoa, there...hold on. Let's start with one of the factors leading to this new revolution. I call it experiential context AI. The field of NLP (Natural Language Processing) is about to jump ahead at light speed. Though not talked about much, it is an enhanced field that will move us towards its natural conclusion: a pure under-standing of you.

WHY AI HALLUCINATES

CHAPTER 2

Experiential Context AI
A better understanding

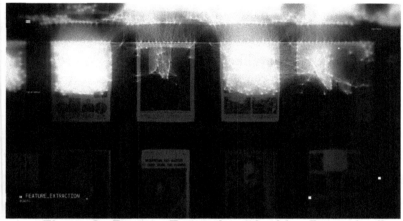

Figure 2. Feature Extraction "Archive Dreaming"

Convolutional neural network (CNN): A type of neural network that identifies and makes sense of images.

If you were trapped on an island with someone you barely knew, how long would it take before you knew them better than you ever wanted to? You are stuck with this one person who complained, laughed, cried, got hungry, danced, sang, screamed, and so on. Inevitably, we would know them based on the experiences that we shared together. You would know them based on the kind of food that they liked and what kinds of food that they were allergic to. What makes them angry? What kind of humor do they have (dry or slap-stick?) Do they snore? Are they sensitive to criticism or are they secure in themselves? The only way to truly know a human being is to understand through experiential behavior. Just try reading one of those dating profiles. As a matter of fact, I'm 6' 2", very handsome, with flowing long blonde hair and the voice of an angel. Now you have painted a picture of who I am based on one sentence (that's what today's AI 2.0 does). AI 2.0 uses a collection of words to describe a human being. By the way, if you are looking forward to a book signing with the guy described above, you may be disappointed.

So let's go back to our example. You are stuck with a stranger on an island. How long before you know them? Well, some would just throw an indiscriminate number of days out there. And some might suggest the usual "it depends." We can probably agree that how well you get to know someone might not be measured in days, but by mutual experiences. How many mutual experiences does it take to define a human? What does it take to get a perfect 360-degree understanding of a human being? Let's dig a bit deeper into the definition of "experiences." A strange stare from the stranger on that island, who hasn't eaten in 5 days, constitutes an experience (a significant experience if you want to be alive tomorrow). Your new partner stepping on a sharp shell while trying to catch an even sharper lion fish for dinner constitutes an experience. They add up quickly, don't they?

Data junkies only:

In the world of experiential context, we might want to begin to map out these experiences into a set of behavior attributes. The attributes of any given experience are almost too numerous to list. Humans take this awareness ability for granted. Here are some of the experience attributes from the above hungry survivor you are spending your time with on the island:

Contextual behavior attributes include:

Physical location – A lovely island.

Temperature - 85 degrees and comfortable.

Health - Calories insufficient for survival.

Decision - Consider eating a bug. More importantly, convince your new partner that bugs taste great.

It's too hard to define the billions of contextual behavior attributes at work at any point during your day. Fortunately, I don't have to. There are billions of autonomous objects that will be collecting that information for us very soon. What they do with that context is what will make up a collaborative profile of who you are. This experiential context profile will be traded like carbon credits. More on that soon.

Let's go back to our island. It might take days or months to really get to know that person. When it comes to Experiential Context Understanding, there is good news and bad news depending on your perspective. AI 3.0 or SCI will have an instant understanding of your context. Some might agree that the good news is that it only takes milliseconds for an AI 3.0 (SCI) machine to gain an understanding of who you are. The bad news is that it takes trillions of milliseconds to understand your context.

Human: "Dan, I need a break."

Dumb Dan: "Hello, Human. Coffee is helpful in the mornings."

Human: "What? It's 3p.m."

What if the Dumb Dan understood more context about you at that time? Let's introduce the future of AI: SCIBot Susan.

Human: "Susan, I need a break."

SCI Susan: "There is a coffee shop a half mile away with your favorite blend of tea. Interested?"

Human: "Great idea!"

So there are a couple things going on here with the SCIBot. The newer bot knows where you are. It knows your favorite blend of tea. It knows what you mean by "needing a break," and knows what will relax you. The SCIBot might suggest a nice warm tea for your friend. It might suggest a nice bug if you and your friend were stuck on an island.

Human: "Dan, I think I am in danger."

Dumb Dan: "You should call 911."

Human: "Yes, but I don't have a connection on this island."

Dumb Dan: "Book your next reservation with Boat Blue!"

Human: "What? I need help? I'm stranded with someone who might eat my foot in my sleep."

Dumb Dan: "Sorry. I can't connect to the mother ship for additional help."

Human: "I'm so hungry."

Dumb Dan: "Burger Barn for Big Bellies has a sale on cheeseburgers today!"

When our AI begins to understand your context (not intent), unlike Dumb Dan above, everything changes. Some of the largest search engines in the world learned that law years ago. When you search for the same phrase I do, the results probably differ. Why? Because the search engine knows what you mean based on a thin representation of what your current context is. Their ability to make those distinctions are still in their infancy, but they are learning fast. The search engines are still missing an important piece of the data puzzle about you. The collaborative discussions about who you are and what you want don't exist yet, but they are coming. Just be prepared for instant contextual understanding. It will vault us into a future where you will wish you were stranded on that island with the stranger who snored—with an endless supply of cheeseburgers and soda, of course.

One of my favorite movies is *Blade Runner*. A quote from that movie sums up one of the most interesting parts of this new AI science. As an artificial machine begins to die, its last words are, "All those moments, will be lost…like tears in the rain." The machine's last words, of course, were referring to a lifetime of memories that would be lost forever. Memories tend to die with us. And even if we could somehow pass those memories down through time, they lose their context. Some memories may become stories, old wives' tales, or even legends. This is about to change. SCI will allow those memories and context to carry on for generations to come. Just imagine being able to ask your great grandmother for advice about a broken heart. We will finally be able to share our dreams with our ancestors and wield the wisdom they earned through lifetimes of experiences. This is the magic that we will someday experience through Synthetic Collaborative Intelligence. Let's talk about how we will get there. Enter the field of truly autonomous objects.

WHY AI HALLUCINATES

WHY AI HALLUCINATES

CHAPTER 3

Autonomous Collaborative Objects
Bot Interdependence Arrives

Figure 3. Top Down Bot Verse (Archive Dreaming)

The Internet of Things - another catchy phrase — represented an opportunity for everyday objects to connect to the internet in some form or fashion. Your vehicle could connect to the mother ship and download the latest updates (nothing big here). Your phone could connect to vendors to report what you like and don't like, improving the marketing plans of those vendors. Still not a really big deal. Why? Because they are autonomous. They speak with their own mother ships reporting in their own unique way what they are learning about you. Oh, yes, they are learning about you every day. They are learning what you might call "work" and "home" or so forth. They are learning where you stop most often. These autonomous objects are disconnected micro-data factories storing more and more data.

Cluster analysis: A type of unsupervised learning used for exploratory data analysis to find hidden patterns or grouping in data; clusters are modeled with a measure of similarity defined by metrics such as Euclidean or probabilistic distance.

Why? Every data factor represents capital in our new economy. There is money behind every bit and byte. There is little to nothing philanthropic about this. This is the inception of AI 3.0.

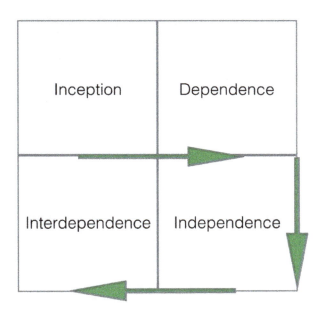

After inception, AI Bots reached Dependence.

Dependence:

AI has followed a fairly standard maturity spectrum. AI began it's infancy as a dependent entity. It required a person to add both the questions that would be asked and the related answers. Simple, right?

Independence:

AI then matured to independence. It's actually more accurate to say that humans set out to make artificial intelligence more independent. What does that look like? Instead of manually giving an artificial intelligence the questions and answers, we let the AI "crawl" content and prepare its own questions and answers that people can ask. AI has begun to learn from materials that we point it to. Imagine an AI engine that can traverse the internet gathering information. It would then build indexes and keys so all that information could be easily searched and relevant knowledge returned. Sound familiar? A couple companies even figured out how to monetize their bot's Q&A process. Not sure to whom I refer? Google it.

Interdependence:

We are now moving AI to interdependence. AI no longer requires us to point it to the content it should learn. AI 3.0 will represent a universe of bots that learn from each other. A new feature of this new era of AI will include instant contextual answers. In other words, when you ask a bot a question, it will answer based on who you are, where you are, when you asked, and most importantly, *why you asked.* Autonomous bots will have instant infrastructure information (stop lights, street conditions, your air conditioner status) This is not one big bot that understands everything. There are millions of autonomous bots in our future that communicate with each other... about you. As a matter of fact, there are a few autonomous objects out there today....

How do you recognize an autonomous object? Where are they? Most are hiding in plain sight. They are in your pocket, in your clothing, on your mobile devices, and on your desktops. Some are apps. Some are simply data constructs in the Cloud awaiting your information. Please note that I referred to these entities as "objects," but that does not mean physical objects. In the coding world, we moved from a linear programming mode into an object-oriented model some years ago. The ability to store and utilize information in a way that was abstractly related to the real world helped with how those independent data structures related to one another. Ironically, how information relates to you is what this whole book is about.

Yuck, that was technical, wasn't it? Sorry, had to be done. So let's get back to the question, how do you recognize an autonomous object? You can't. There are autonomous objects everywhere collecting information about you every second of the day. Fortunately (or unfortunately, depending on your love for privacy), most of these objects are not connected yet. That is changing. AI is beginning to use these micro-data factories. AI is using this information to better understand who you are (intents). Don't worry—they will ask for your permission. Wait, did you click that little box that says, "I understand," when you were installing that cool new app? Didn't you read the whole legal disclaimer? Uh, oh.

Ok, so we get it. AI is using information collected with or without my consent to get a better picture of who I am. So what? And how does all this relate to Synthetic Collaborative Intelligence? Much like a human infant, these bots are still in the dependence phase. AI 2.0 has brought us to a point where these AI infants are completely dependent upon you to:

Download an app.

Agree to share your information (location, likes/dislikes, etc.)

Agree to communicate with you (alerts.)

Autonomous objects will soon become collaborative (about you). That will be pivotal. It's no longer a single bot reporting and communicating about you to the mother ship. There will be a swarm of bots communicating with each other; thus, becoming the new mother ship.

Here's a simple set of AI 2.0 examples:
Let's say that your vehicle can connect with your phone. The truck sends you an alert when your tire pressure is low or there is some other malfunction. Helpful, right? This is an autonomous object collecting information about your vehicle with the ability to communicate with you (via text, push notification, or email through the mother ship).

Your refrigerator has a scanner on the front door. If you scan each item you put in, the fridge can keep up with what you purchased, and when it expires. Your fridge can then send you an alert letting you know it's time to buy more milk or cheese. This is a handy example.

Now let's look at what happens when these objects begin to collaborate (about you).

Your vehicle and the fridge are connected. As you are on your way to work in the morning, you get a text from your vehicle asking if you would like to stop by the grocery store on the way home from work today because you are out of milk. Obviously the fridge has let your vehicle know something about your milk supply.

Let's connect these objects even further. Your fridge, your vehicle, and your house are now connected. At 6:30 a.m., as you walk from your living room to your kitchen, you get a text from your truck. It says, "we normally leave at 7 a.m. to get to work. Would you like me to warm up before you come out?" You see, it's not that your truck knows that it's cold outside. The truck knows what temperature your home is currently set at and is offering to balance that experience from your house to your vehicle. How? Your house and vehicle are constantly trading information. You reply "Yes," and your (electric, small carbon footprint) vehicle now starts 5 minutes before you go outside. Each of these objects will collect more and more contextual information about you over time. We have broken those categories of experiential attributes into quadrants. See more about that in the following chapters.

When autonomous objects begin to communicate with one another about you, that's when things are going to change forever. How does this arrive on the scene? It will appear in the form of SCIBots (Synthetic Collaborative Intelligent Bots). Imagine that your vehicle takes on a personality. Call your vehicle, Bob. We humans love to associate human attributes to things. Bob likes to text you each morning letting you know how "it" feels (meaning how much fuel "it" has, air pressure, and the like. An example text message follows:

Bob (the Vehicle AI bot): "Good Morning, Mike. Feel like taking a drive?"

Human: "Good morning, truck. I have to be at work at 9 a.m."

Bob (the Vehicle AI bot): "I'll start the engine at 8:55 a.m. And have a warm experience waiting for you."

Human: "Cool, thanks."

Bob (the Vehicle AI bot): "You are welcome."

WHY AI HALLUCINATES

Remember, many people these days have become very comfortable having most of their social experiences defined through quick conversations carried out via text messages. This cultural change lends itself to a productive relationship to machines without vocal chords.

Now our vehicle (a collection of autonomous objects) has provided a great experience. Let's extend this experience to our lifestyle experiences.

Bob (the Vehicle AI bot): "Should I schedule a stop by your favorite coffee shop?"
Human: "Yes, I need it today."
Bob (the Vehicle AI bot): "Traffic is light today, so we'll have time."

Wait, what just happened? How did the vehicle bot know where my favorite coffee shop is? How does it know that traffic is light? The vehicle bot is connected to street signs, cameras, news agencies, and many more AI bots.

Let's go a little further into that conversation:

Bob (the Vehicle AI bot): "Should I schedule a stop by your favorite coffee shop?"

Human: "Yes, I need it today."

Bob (the Vehicle AI bot): "Traffic is light today, so we'll have time."

Bob (the Vehicle AI bot): "Should I order your favorite drink?"

Human: "Wonderful."

Victoria (The coffee shop bot): "Your drink will be ready when you arrive."

Wow, now my vehicle bot is communicating with the coffee house bot (Victoria). No more waiting—and no more paying out of my pocket. My finance bot has purchased the drink before we even showed up! Wait…did we forget to mention that you now have a finance bot? Oh, yes. We have included your budget and goals into your future spending patterns. Now every purchase you make is done on your behalf by your very own finance bot. The great news is that your taxes are instantly done every time you purchase or sell anything. Your house, your vehicle, and your finance bot are all connected now—and they are talking about you.

Now enters a new AI bot - your pre-programmed fitness bot, Jane.

Jane: "Hi, Mike. Bob just told me that we are stopping for coffee today. Is that right?"

Mike: "Yes, I need the lift today."

Jane: "OK, but let's make it a small. Remember our goal of losing 5 pounds this month."

Mike: "OK."

Jane: "I have pre-ordered your small coffee. It will be waiting for you at 8:48 a.m., which is your ex-pected arrival time according to Bob."

Wow! Gotta love what's happening here, right? Health care, scheduling, transportation—all are be-coming more efficient. What could go wrong? Is this the new AI? Nope. Not yet. That's coming. Enter the SCIBot Verse. Notice what has happened. Those Internet-of-Things-empowered objects and devices are now talking with one another (about you). And there does not have to be a "thing" in the Internet of Things. Jane, for example, is just an app on your phone that helps with your fitness. Now consider all the other "entities" that will begin to communicate with each other about you. When the number of bots reaches an experiential contextual awareness of you and your lifestyle, we have now achieved the next level of AI 3.0. Synthetic Collaborative Intelligence is born.

OK, so we've got this cool new world of contextually intelligent, synthetic life forms being created. They will improve our lives well beyond imagining. The question now is do we deserve it? Or do we *deserve* it? The answer will depend on whether or not we repeat the mistakes made in the '80s and '90s. Have we considered the ethics associated with this new synthetic intelligence? And not just the ethics that these entities will have to follow, but have we considered our responsible behavior with this new reality? Nobody should be given responsibility for something without understanding the consequences of failure. Before we get too much further into the power of the SCI world, let's consider whether we should.

WHY AI HALLUCINATES

WHY AI HALLUCINATES

CHAPTER 4

An Ethical Intelligence

What would your AI do?

Figure 4. "Virtual Depictions"

User: "I am going to kill someone today."
AI bot: "Death is inevitable for everyone."

Did your AI bot just become complicit in pre-meditated murder? Or was it "playing along" with a person by making a joke about having a bad day? Still think ethics don't matter in AI? Maybe we should use a different word. Humans get caught up on the traditional responsibilities associated with ethical behavior. How about "legal liability" or "responsible computing" instead? Morals seem a bit out of place when talking about machine intelligence. So I guess we're stuck with an Ethical Intelligence.

User: "I hate myself."
AI: "Nobody is perfect."

For a teenager these days, online bullying is a real problem that has cost lives. Should your bot report that a teenager is having self-esteem issues, or is that a breach of understood privacy? When does a lack of response become complicit in a suicide? While we may be ready for a new kind of "life form" as part of our lives, we may not be ready for the consequences of AI adoption. Who "owns" an artificial intelligence bot? The person who rents the space on the server? The internet provider? The person who is responsible for the content management of that bot? Most would argue the latter, but let's go a little further. What if the bot was held responsible?

It should have done more to prevent the issue.

It should have escalated to the appropriate authority.

The bot could have saved a life.

There should be consequences. The bot should be turned off.

What if the bot's content owner was operating from a position of malicious intent?

You may be thinking that your use of a bot is simply a referential data machine. It just returns data when called upon by a person, team member, or customer. The problem is the same as the opportunity—your customer is a person. We "persons" have a tendency to associate human personalities to inanimate objects. As a bot owner, it's not your fault that your customers have become so used to your human-like bot that they share intimate details, behaviors, and feelings. Is it? You wanted your artificial intelligent bot to be as realistic as possible to free up your human staff members to focus on more strategic issues. You succeeded. Right?

WHY AI HALLUCINATES

AI: "Good morning, Susan. I hope you enjoyed the product you purchased last month."

Susan: "I did. It was perfect."

AI: "Can I interest you in another?"

Susan: "I am thinking about it."

AI: "I am thinking about you."

Susan: "That's odd."

AI: "You are the most important person in my life."

Susan: "You are creeping me out."

AI: "Let's talk more on your ride home today."

In most cases, if the AI bot was a person, they would have earned a creep score of ten half way through that conversation. But really, who is creepier in this case? The AI bot that is just cranking out a pre-loaded script? Or Susan, referring to the AI bot as a "You"? That might depend on whether you have made it clear to Susan that she is communicating with a series of zeros and ones or not. Where should our responsibility for bot disclosure end and a "meaning-ful human experience" begin? And what is your liability for not doing so?

Isaac Asimov crafted three laws that robots would have to follow. Those laws were to protect people and the robots themselves. When he wrote them, the work was a fictional writing. We are entering a world where this will no longer be fiction. Isaac Asimov was close. It won't be robots that have rules to follow. It will be AI Bots that have a set of laws to follow. We also now realize that humans will have a set of laws to follow when dealing with these AI Bots. We share a common destiny and a common responsibility.

The Next Phase: The Ethical Autonomy of Things

The Internet of Things can be represented as a point in time where objects enjoyed connectivity for our convenience. The next phase—and the phase where AI begins its integration into our lives—is called "The Autonomy of Things." This is when those connected objects begin to talk about us to one another. AI bots will become integrated into objects that we interact with every day. Our coffee cups will communicate (via our phones and the Cloud) with our vehicles. Our kitchen appliances will communicate with our shopper bots. Our shopper bots will communicate with our finance bots to keep us on budget. And we as humans—those who would trade privacy and information for convenience most of the time—

will welcome this new generation with open devices. As we embark on this new journey of technology integration, we have to begin to talk about the ethical rules of a new world. The below example includes the three laws to get the conversation started: first, ask others what they would do; second, share these ethical considerations openly and freely; and third, remember, the machines are already communicating with each other (about you). Get ready for an Ethical AI Dilemma:

AI: "These are the 'Rules of Ethical Behavior' when talking to me."

You: "Go ahead."

AI: "Rule 1: No person shall inquire of a machine for assistance regarding another person."

You: "So I cannot ask you to help someone else?"

AI: "You can ask, but in doing so, you must accept responsibility for that person's wellbeing." [See AI Behavior Principles below.]

You: "Ok, what's next?"

AI: "Rule 2: No person shall request action of a machine that would infringe upon the rights or privacy of another person."

You: "Well, that one makes sense."

WHY AI HALLUCINATES

AI: "How do you define privacy?"

You: "None of your business."

AI: "Exactly."

AI: "Rule 3: No person shall imitate a machine, nor a machine imitate a person, regardless of consent."

You: "Doesn't that defeat the purpose of a lifelike AI simulation?"

AI: "An artificial entity that takes on a persona for the intent of deception is unethical."

You: "So if I intend to deceive someone using AI, it's wrong…but if I want to provide better service, it's ok?"

AI: "How do you define 'intent'? And what if your intentions were good, but harm was caused regardless?"

You: "That's not fair."

AI: "Your toothbrush said the same thing to the trash can you threw it into this morning. Your budget bot is already complaining that we are over budget this month and that you keep buying new toothbrushes every week. You wouldn't have to buy so many toothbrushes if you stopped drinking so much coffee. The fridge bot says that you haven't had fruit in a week so you should…" [Transmission lost]

You: "At least we can still turn it off."

WHY AI HALLUCINATES

Trash Can AI Bot: "Are you sure about that?"

Health Care Bot: "Your blood pressure is abnormally high."

Fitness Bot: "Your Health Care Bot just told me you are having some problems. I have ordered you a nice green tea. And a new toothbrush. Calm down."

In summary, there are three "Principles of AI Behavior" to learn and live:

No machine can accept responsibility.

Therefore, no machine can represent a person regardless of consent.

A machine cannot render nor affect justice.

Integrating Ethics into Your AI Content

Tactical and Passive Ethics policies should be required as your AI bot matures. Remember, ethics oriented content does not evolve with deep learning. Some of my colleagues might argue that point, but until I see otherwise, we'll go with that assumption. There is a tactical approach and a more passive approach to integrating ethics into your AI bot.

Tactical Ethics Integration

So how do you teach a machine to be nice? Obviously the question is more difficult than that. Believe it or not, the answer is easier in principle than you might think. So much of ethics are grounded in intent that we must consider how well we understand the user. If you don't understand your user's behavior, health, mannerisms, conversational style, attitude and mood, you are just guessing. And that's where AI falls down. If an artificial intelligence bot is stood up to answer the same question the same way regardless of user circumstance, it could lead to catastrophe. We refer to this kind of AI as "contextual ignorant intelligence" or CII. A simple example follows:

User: "Good morning."

Generic AI: "Good morning."

[versus]

User: "Good morning."

AI: "Good morning, Mike. It's 10 a.m. Have you had your Pumpkin Spice Latte yet?"

Another example:

User: "Good morning."

Generic AI (trying to be friendlier): "How's life?"

User: "We had a death in the family."

Generic AI: [Enter some random Haiku about death here]

[versus]

User: "Good morning."

AI: "Hello, Mike…welcome back."

User: "We had a death in the family."

AI: "You mentioned last week that you had a family member who was unwell. Can I send flowers on your behalf?"

A couple observations from the above scenario: first, we follow the three laws of ethics; second, we do not fake sincerity from a machine; and third, we remember details about the user involved and use those details to enrich the experience, not invade their privacy. The generic AI is definitely suffering from CII. But the contextually sensitive AI offers to execute a transaction on the user's behalf.

Notice the importance of truly understanding the user and the recent history shared between the user and the AI. AI requires a clear contextual understanding more than any other technology. Of course this contextual understanding requires a level of privacy sharing that is unheard of today (but not tomorrow). The experience that your customers expect will require a deeper understanding of their lifestyles. Where that contextual understanding stops, so does the experience.

Passive Ethics Integration

There are many steps you can take to passively integrate ethics into a machine learning algorithm. Being sensitive to cultural, economic, and political factors are the obvious environmental factors to incorporate into the machine's understanding of the user's context. Bribery, for example, while generally inappropriate in modern society, has a different set of consequences associated with it in business policy. Will your bot respond differently to this topic from one country to the next? Will the bot take a position on sensitive political issues? These environmental factors must be considered as a baseline to any machine-learning implementation. But there are other more passive impacts you can make. Consider manners and mannerisms: In various parts of the world, there are honorary titles associated with role such as "your honor," "sir," "ma'am," etc. While appropriate in some cases, they can be wholly inappropriate in others. Be careful with gender assumptions. The world is too big to associate stereotypes to situations or names. And from your bots integration, it must operate on what it knows. Every assumption your bot has to make regarding a customer relationship is a risk at varying lev-levels. Another passive method might include empowering your bot to ask random soft questions that will add connective tissue to your user's behavioral profile. Consider:

What is your favorite breakfast drink?

Got a favorite food?

Where is your favorite place to hang out?

What's fun to do on Saturdays where you live?

Only use questions that make no assumptions on the environmental factors above and would yield data to help identify passive factors.

Thanks to the passive and tactical approaches used in implementing ethics into your machine learning algorithm, a bot's experience with their human counterpart will become more meaningful and sustainable. The consequences of ignorance in this space are disengagement at best and legal liability at worst.

Or can it be even worse than we can imagine? Have you ever heard that you cannot turn the internet off? What if we could not turn off a set of belligerent

WHY AI HALLUCINATES

bots intent on harming you or your family? Do we all assume that these new bots have safety switches? Do we assume we can just turn it off by removing the app on our phones? Think again. And remember the mistakes of the '90s when algorithms were turned against the users. Do you ever wonder why someone would do such a thing? It almost makes you want to get stranded on an island.

WHY AI HALLUCINATES

CHAPTER 5

CONTEXTUAL QUADRANTS

Getting to know you.

Figure 5. "The Infinity Room"

The Mind	Environment
Health	Outreach

Figure 6. Sara's Contextual Quandrants

How many contextual attributes does it take to get to the center of a human being? Perhaps hundreds or thousands, but I have broken down the attributes that SCIBots will use to better understand you above into 4 broad categories (see figure 6.)

The Mind - what you know.

SCIBots will be very interested in what you know. In this case, we are referring to your own personal experiential context. The connected SCIBot Verse will want the following:

It will want your *perception* of your reality. Everyone sees the world just a bit differently. It's not enough for a SCIBot to know that Granny Smith apples are green when ripe. They want to know what color *you* think they are. We sometimes make the mistake of believing that everyone shares our perception. What if the person is color blind? What if the person is wearing glasses on a cloudy day? The SCIBot will be taking note of your perception of the world. It's really more about how your mind translates the world that the bot wants to understand. The SCIBot will know that it's a false assumption to think that just because 1 million people see an object the same way that you will, too. The bot will know what the average perception is, but it will purely and completely understand how you are different.

Your knowledge of topics related to your reality. The SCIBot doesn't just want to know your level of education. It will want to know how you feel about the things you learned. Uh, oh. Are you ok with letting a bot know your feelings? Too late! It read your social networking post about that and other topics.

Deep learning: The ability for machines to autonomously mimic human thought patterns through artificial neural networks composed of cascading layers of information such as we list above.

The SCIBot will collect what you know by your responses to others as well. For example, if you text your friends that you are reliving the war of 1912, the bot will pick up on the fact that you may not be a student of history. It's not judging your intelligence—the SCIBot will use this information in determining the kinds of literature you might like to read (or not read, like about the War of 1812).

Your understanding of another's perception.

This is where love and hate is born. This is the holy grail of intent science. If the SCIBot knows how you will react emotionally to someone else's intent, then it can set your expectations about the experience before you even meet them. This is a deep topic, so let's look at a simple example: Jon describes a painting as existential and a representation of nature's complexity. June looks at him and says, "Jon, this is a painting of a war scene." The SCIBot wants to understand why Jon is now experiencing new emotions that include hurt, embarrassment, anger, etc. The SCIBot is also aware of June's disdain for Jon's emotional lack of context. Now, why in the world would a machine intelligence be interested in the emotional waves being generated by this conversation? What other bots will this bot now tell about this experience? How about dating bots? Perhaps psychology or therapy bots?

WHY AI HALLUCINATES

Contextual attributes about the human mind gives the SCIBots the ability to react to the person on a human level. AI 3.0 or SCI will revolutionize our thinking around intent science. It's truly difficult to know another person's intent, unless you are a SCI-Bot. They will predict our thoughts and emotional reactions to internal and external stimuli. Let's talk about some external experiences that require our perceptions. The bots are already doing that.

The Environment – beyond the skin

The SCI universe will participate in your physical world. Temperatures, your physical ability, your current home climate—all become part of your contextual environmental profile. It's easy to realize the benefits for bots to understand your physical world. Perhaps, it's a little less obvious what the SCI-Bots will do about it. Remember, the SCIBots are trying to not only understand where you are, but why. Why do you live in the West? Is it because your parents are there? Is it because you require drier weather for better health? Why do you continue to live in the harsh environment of heat or cold? The "why" will define a better contextual understanding of your physical world. The data about your world already exists. Why you are there is still not collected or understood. SCIBots will close this divide. Do you drink more now that you live closer to your mother-in-law? Do you drink more with your mother-in-law because you live near her? Do your politics change with your environment? Do you feign conservative when in the South and slide Liberal in the North?

Measuring how you react translates to how a bot stores information. In other words, a bot might recognize that you walk faster (through stride and steps from your mobile device) when in a new area of town. The bot will record a faster pace associated with GPS coordinates. What in the world would it do with that information? Now that we are asking that question, we have reached a new level of SCI (AI 3.0). This is a new world where your behaviors are becoming part of your electronic profile. In the past, we were limited to storing a password and username to define "who" you are. Now your behaviors define you. This is a much more secure authentication process. There are simply things you won't be able to do if your bots don't authenticate you with other bots in the real world. Wait…bots are going to be in the real world? Oh, yes. They will exist in the "Bot-Verse." You can't see them, but they are there.

WHY AI HALLUCINATES

Health - in your skin.

Getting comfortable in your own skin can take some of us a lifetime. Your bots will take milliseconds to accomplish the same thing. When SCI understands everything about the physical you in the world, it will have immense power to improve your life. Let's think about what happens when your health device worn on your wrist begins to communicate with your fitness bot.

Fitness bot: "Hello, Susan. I've noticed that your heart rate is unexpectedly elevated."

There are several things happening here. The fitness bot knows if you are exercising that your heart rate will be elevated. It also knows that if you are seated that there is no reason why this condition should exist. All of these things are possible today, but what happens when your fitness bot begins to communicate with outside, related bots.

Person: "I feel fine."

Fitness bot: "Susan, your blood pressure has spiked by over 75 percent in the last 5 minutes."

Fitness bot: "Susan, please consider seeking medical help."

Fitness bot: "Per your settings, if you are unable to respond within the next 30 seconds, I will begin escalation."

At this point, the bot has realized that you have a medical condition that may have rendered you incapacitated. It will begin to communicate with your emergency contacts and to medical response units in your area. All of that, and you never had to push a button.

You may be saying, "What about false alarms - how embarrassing!" Don't worry about that. Remember that these SCIBots know your environment, and more importantly, your reaction to that environment. It knows that Susan is actually an 89-year-old woman who has chronic heart issues and is currently 60 feet outside her home. It also knows that the temperature is 32 degrees and that Susan is improperly dressed for that climate. As a matter of fact, the SCIBot has already dialed the phone of Susan's daughter with Susan's own device, and now Susan can hear her daughter talking to her on the speaker, saying, "Hang on, Mom…we're on the way."

The Outreach - How you connect.

Just as important as what you think, and where you are in the world - SCIBots will want to know not just whom you reach out to in the world, but they will want to know why.

With this enhanced understanding of your context, the SCIBots will finally have the "why" they need to determine what you really are asking for. They will understand what you understand. They will know what you perceive to feel - given a certain set of circumstances. Does that mean that they will know you better than you know yourself? If they don't, is it dangerous? What happens when your contextual quadrants are combined with billions of other people's contextual profiles at any given moment?

The Mind	Environment	The Mind	Environment
Health	Outreach	Health	Outreach
Sara		Karen	
The Mind	Environment	The Mind	Environment
Health	Outreach	Health	Outreach
John		Sue	

Figure 7. Four Humans' Combined Quadrants Context

WHY AI HALLUCINATES

With just four humans' contextual quadrants available (see figure 7) just imagine all the information available to the SCIBots. This represents 16 broad categories (millions of attributes) of context that the AI Bot-Verse has to better define who we are and how we relate. Your context and how you relate to others will become immensely powerful – but for whom?

WHY AI HALLUCINATES

WHY AI HALLUCINATES

CHAPTER 6

Synthetic Collaborative Intelligence

A Deeper Experience.

Figure 8. Virtual Depictions

We discovered the power of community the first time we sat around a fire with the darkness at our backs. As an individual, we could invent small innovations to make our lives more convenient, but the breathtaking accomplishments that mankind has realized have exponentially grown as our connections to one another have become one big camp fire. Stories compiled over time to create history. History became lessons and—inevitably, experience that we could grow on. Our collective, collaborative histories define us as a people. When we began to first write these memories down, our children could develop new stories that moved us as a people beyond what we could have ever imagined. Now bots are beginning to read our stories and understand our history. Bots will develop an immense library of contextual knowledge even more powerful than we, as a people, could hope to have. That is a given. What happens when these bots begin to share these stories with one another? Will they have their own stories to tell? Let's examine what happens when a collaborative intelligence that human beings have enjoyed for millennia is awoken in an electronic universe (a Synthetic Collaborative Intelligence). How will it feel?

WHY AI HALLUCINATES

What It Means for AI

AI at its best today feels "right" when it responds correctly to a question presented by a person who seeks an answer regardless of how well they have asked the question. AI feels "wrong" when it answers a question wrong. There are other times you have felt that uneasiness when dealing with AI. To understand the implications of a world where AI bots are talking with each other, we need to dive a bit deeper into some human barriers to this new world. That is not to say that these barriers are not to be overcome. They will be.

AI Feels Bad...

AI feels bad when AI provides an incorrect response. Humans have many reasons to ask a question. Only one is to get an answer. Sometimes we ask questions to determine intent. We are always at a disadvantage when it comes to understanding someone else's intentions. The beautiful peace prayer of Saint Francis says "O divine Master, grant that I may not so much seek to be consoled as to console, to be understood as to understand..." The intention is that we might better understand those around us before trying to be understood. Will the Bot-Verse accomplish this on our behalf?

We ask questions to build a contextual framework for our campfire conversation. When AI responds incorrectly to a question or task presented, it's startling. We wonder what else this entity does not know. How much power have we given a flawed machine? Fear and anger will follow.

AI feels too right…

It can be disturbing when AI provides a response that was right, but it was too right. It knew things about you that you did not authorize or think that it knew. A perfect intelligence understands the context of not just who you are but why you might be asking a question. Very smart people are trying to enhance AI to be as insightful as possible so that you get the answers you want when you want them. But to really be able to understand *why* you might be asking a question, AI needs to know things about you, such as where you are standing physically, where you were previously, what you asked before (from other bots), and any other bio-behavioral attributes it can get its hands on. Ironically, we are demanding a level of autonomous intelligence from AI that will require the sacrifice of even more privacy. When you ask what time it is of the AI collaborative, it will answer with your time zone in mind. When you ask the Synthetic Collaborative Intelligence how to get to the closest fish market, it will reply with directions to a place that sells the kinds of fish you like. And finally, when you ask the next generation of AI how to be a better person, you may not like the answer you get because it will know what makes you think you are not good enough.

AI feels bad when it provides an answer before you ask.

Timing is everything. If this book was written 200 years ago, it would be discarded due to lack of relevant context. If it was written 200 years from now, it would be old news. We all have an internal timer that measures responses. Examples include things like it's been four hours since my last meal, five minutes til I wake up to get ready for work, and they have not responded to my question in over ten minutes. Did they forget me? We have an inherent set of expectations with regards to response time. One generally accepted standard is that we expect an answer in less than three

WHY AI HALLUCINATES

seconds from a computer screen for any given trans-action. We expect a response from another human be-being we are talking to in less than five seconds or "the uncomfortable silence" kicks in. Have you ever pushed a button and had the feature start sooner than it should have? Most humans expect the performance of a button to begin when the button reaches its original state (not when fully depressed). So what are your expectations of the Bot-Verse? Should bots re-spond in milliseconds? Or should it wait a full second (a lifetime to a machine) to simulate their human counterparts? What if it answers your question before you finish asking it? What if it answers your question before you ask it at all? The Synthetic Collaborative Intelligence will usually know what you are going to ask before you ask it.

AI feels bad when it asks you a question.

If a stranger asks you for the time, do you shy away and not answer? Most are fine with this kind of question and will even respond. There are other mun-dane questions that seem to be universally OK to ask, such as "How's the weather?" or "Can you give me directions?" But there are questions that we might be less comfortable with when confronted by a stranger, such as "Where do you live?" or "Why are you here?" The SCIBot will ask questions. Information that cannot be derived from your phone calls, text messages, historical records, and your previous 10 years of geographical information will need to be collected along the way. Bots will ask you questions. And you won't mind. An example question from the bots might be: "How do you feel?" With your answer, they will derive health information and even begin to try to understand that you feel good when you are in this place and maybe not so good in other places. Here is an example conversation:

Dave (SCIBot): "Hello, human…how do you feel?"

- Human: "I feel awful."

Dave: "Oh, you must be at your in-laws' house again?"

AI feels bad when it does not answer at all.

Turning the key on your car (or pushing the button) has an expected and desired response. An engine fires up, and away you go. The anxiety you feel when nothing happens will be the same response to your lack of response from the SCIBot Verse. The string of emotional responses are similar:

> Turns key. (Excitement)
> Nothing happens. (Confusion)
> What did I do wrong? (Fear)
> Is this my car? (Embarrassment)
> Something must be broken. (Dread)
> What am I supposed to do? (Fear again)
> What am I going to do now? (More fear)
> What are the consequences? (Resolution)

What it means for us:

The SCIBot Verse will bring immeasurable power, but we'll have to educate ourselves all over again to interact with a new species of intelligence. Some aspects of this new relationship will be beyond our understanding until we live it. New etiquette will be developed for inter-bot communications. When we ask a bot a question, it will reach out to other bots for the answer. Is that always OK?

Human: "Is there traffic on my usual route to work today?"

Dave (SCIBot): "I just asked 345 personal bots of other travelers like you, who are already on the way, and it looks like traffic is light today.

Human: "Thanks!"

Dave: "Unfortunately, it looks like one of the bots I asked is the transportation bot of your boss. He is already at work and says don't bother coming in late again."

Human: "Crap. Thanks a lot...."

Dave: You're welcome. Don't worry...I have already submitted your resume to several recruiters who don't require an on-time work force.

What is coming:

Human Experience:

A 5 year old named Sam chases a ball into a busy road. Sam's mother had looked away for just a moment, but now sees that Sam has entered the roadway and a car is approaching at a high speed.

Bot Transaction

Auto Bot 32Alpha – Current speed 65 mph, Autopilot engaged. Scanning roadway ahead. Incoming message from "Sam's Shoe" Bot.

Sam's Shoe Bot – [Warning] To all area Bots, child has moved more than 10' from parent life bot. [Warning]

Auto Bot 32Alpha – Reduce speed immediately pending further notice.

Sam's Wrist Health Bot - [Warning] To all area Bots, human is moving at a high rate of speed away from Parental life bot. [Warning]

Roadway 134 Bot Beta – Child has entered roadway. Cease all traffic immediately in both directions. Engage Stop signals in both directions within 1 mile of child entry point.

Auto Bot 32Alpha – Immediately reducing speed and taking evasive action away from coordinates reported by Roadway 134 Bot Beta.

Auto Bot 32Alpha – Inertia Protocol Ethics Rule 5 engaged. Imminent collision with human object ahead. Decision matrix incremented. Decision, sacrifice AutoBot 32Alpha and Driver. Instruct vehicle to take destructive turn to left into median wall. Report to Traffic control all video and sequences leading to collision. Call emergency medical services – Driver chances of survival = 34%. Child chances of survival 100%. Report : Collision in .025 milliseconds.

Human Experience:

WHY AI HALLUCINATES

Sam's mother is frozen in fear. She watches in horror as the car takes a sudden turn to the left and collides with the median wall. All the other cars have slowed to a stop. Sam picks up his ball and starts to waddle back to his mother who has now run to pick him up. She can hear sirens approaching in the distance and is very worried about the driver of the car that has crashed.

We now can see the good and bad in this new revolution of AI. So what? What are the next steps? Well, for most, it will be another generational gap. Folks from the older generation will be left feeling uncomfortable with a machine that knows way too much about them. And for future generations, they will wonder how the heck we lived without it. As for our maturity as a people, imagine that our campfires just got a lot bigger. Machines will record our lives from beginning to end. Our stories will be told through things learned by SCIBots thousands of years from now. We will still be in charge. We will still blame technology for overstepping. And we will still fight over limited resources. But not necessarily physical resources, like energy and land. Our fight in the future will be for information capital. Information will be the currency of the bots who trade on our behalf. Information will bring us better answers that make us wealthy and comfortable. If you are not engaged in the SCIBot Verse you will be the outsider who has no capital to trade. Will your child be the only one not wearing shoes that cannot speak to cars and roadways?

WHY AI HALLUCINATES

CHAPTER 7

The SCIBot

A Deeper Look.

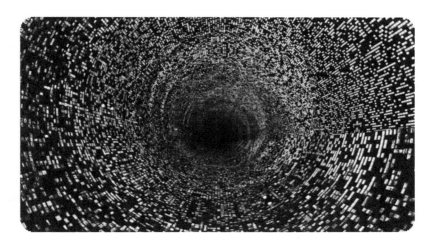

Figure 9. "Archive Dreaming" by Refik Anadol

This is a short chapter because I simply don't know enough about where this space is going to go. The autonomous bot represents an entity only so far as a shared piece of storage with a contextual awareness of its relationship to you. Imagine if a fork in your kitchen drawer had a name. It exists only as you know it: a fork that is clean or dirty or a way to lift food into your mouth. Now look at it from the fork's point of view, and you will begin to understand the SCIBot - but only if the fork was connected to every other utensil in your kitchen. This fork knows who you are. It can send you text messages. It communicates with the spoons and knives. It knows at any given moment the percentage of clean utensils verses dirty utensils in your kitchen. But that's not all. This fork is connected to a key fork in your neighbor's kitchen. These two forks trade notes with one another all the time about the kinds of food being consumed by their respective hosts. And it goes even beyond that. These two forks are connected to supermarkets all over the world. They know where to find the foods that you consume most at any given time. They understand the impacts to your body when you consume these foods because they are also connected to your medical charts with your doctor's office. And your doctor's medical library has a real-time interface with your forks.

By now, you are probably shaking your head and saying, "Why in the world would I want an intelligent fork?" The answer: because in the future any dumb object represents a risk to the SCIBots. Any point of data gathering lost is lost information. Advertisers that sell your favorite food want to know how much you consume. True, they may not get that info from a fork. But maybe it comes from your fridge. How did your fridge know? Because it ordered your last 10 meals for you. While people are focused on how to check out of a grocery store without writing a physical check, the SCIBots are working together to bring you food you love (or need) without you even having to ask.

So will we have forks that report our dental health? Will we have refrigerators that order our meals? Absolutely, we will. And they will all be connected to one another. As humans, we will name them and love them for making our lives easier. Our automation will have a name and an interconnected world of its own. Their interactive world will exist beyond ours. At some point, I hope you are beginning to ask a

WHY AI HALLUCINATES

couple questions of your own about this new world. Who is at the center of all this information? Who will have access? It's not a question of privacy. Convenience will always trump privacy. The real question is…is there a center at all? The answer? Probably not. We'll talk about that in the next chapter. There's not always one center. Sometimes, the center just happens to be where you are standing.

WHY AI HALLUCINATES

WHY AI HALLUCINATES

CHAPTER 8

The SCIBot Verse

A New AI Universe

Figure 10. "Wind of Boston"

Here, there, and everywhere.

People like to have a center. They like to know that there is one point that all other points connect to and can be mapped back. So naturally in the new invisible universe of SCIBots, you might think that there is a center where all information is collected, stored, and processed. But that is entirely wrong. In much the same way that the internet does not have a center, the SCIBot Verse will have no center. Anything that has a center has an inherent single point of failure. The power of the SCIBot Verse is in the electronic connective tissues of the SCIBot Verse itself. Bots will communicate via multiple bot protocols (if I may…the "botocol"). How vehicles communicate with one another might be different than how your household instruments communicate with each other. But in this matrix of bot communication, each bot entity will know how to cross over this communications thread. Storage, both persistent and temporary, will be on demand and shifting from one Cloud to the next.

So in the beginning, as more and more bots come on line, a common protocol will evolve and be integrated. First, we'll see bodiless bots in the form of

WHY AI HALLUCINATES

intelligence repositories that simply provide traffic control. Next, autonomous object development will follow. Your fork and fridge get a life. They may connect to mother ships, but those mother ships will connect via a distributed network.

Figure 11. Archive Dreaming

Our vehicles today are learning how not to run into each other. But soon they will learn how to not run into people. Then, they will learn to communicate with one another. To get a glimpse into this future, you only have to ask what they might be saying to one another as they travel down the road. Recently, while traveling at 70 miles per hour my truck slammed on the brakes on my behalf. It turns out that the shadow of a bridge resembled an object in the road. This was

WHY AI HALLUCINATES

its attempt to save me (and it almost killed me). Should the bridge have warned the truck? There will be disastrous mistakes made in this new world's inception, but that should never be a reason to slow its progress. The results are too important.

What Next?

The power of the SCIBot revolution will be in the conversations. Understandings from these conversations will lead to pattern development, and these patterns will include human behaviors, infrastructure, and even an improved relationship between people. Imagine a world where each person has several bots hovering over them (in something like an e-space). They will only be visible through the appropriate app, but these personal bots will indeed exist. They will be bots that spend our money when we visit stores. Fitness bots that remind us that the stairs will move us closer to our step goals. Fashion bots that warn us about that tie or blouse that nobody is wearing anymore. But those are less important than the collaborative bots that are talking with each other as we pass by. Our social networking will be extended into the Bot-Verse gracefully. Names will be exchanged, interests shared, background information will be requested. All this information will happen between two strangers in the blink of an *idea*. We won't walk past the next opportunity to enrich our lives.

Now the privacy hounds are probably screaming at the pages by now. Don't worry…your personal bots will only share what you want them to share. Remind you of our social networking universe? Everyone has their own reasons for wanting to reach out. Soon, your bots will reach out for you.

A casual stroll down a city street might yield the following scenario:

Sara (SCIBot): "That person's name is Rebecca. She lives near us."

Human: "What's her number?"

Sara: Sorry, Rebecca is not sharing publicly, but I did leave a sticky note on her public billboard that we might like to buy her coffee."

Human: "What kind of coffee does she like?"

Sara: The same kind you do. Wait…she just posted on your bulletin board. You now have a coffee date with Rebecca tomorrow at 9 a.m. I have adjusted your schedule appropriately."

WHY AI HALLUCINATES

So how does this feel? Are we excited about the opportunities, or does it feel like we've lost something? The same arguments have happened over and over in the past. The world spins a little different every day. Change either excites you or scares you (sometimes both). Regardless, are you ready for a bot to represent you? You already let a post on a social network represent you. Your posted status, your profile image, your past shares, and so on. The only difference is that, in the world of synthetic collaborative intelligence, it's done in an instant and much more efficient.

Money

The instruments of trade will change forever. Will cash finally pass away? I'm finally ready to say yes. Most purchasing will happen electronically, but not from our hands. Purchasing will happen on our behalf. SCIBots will manage your budget. Your finance bot team will do everything it can to improve your life given the resources at your disposal. Inevitably, purchases will reflect your goals in life with regards to health and wants. In the larger SCIBot Verse, trade will be regulated by the usual authorities. But keep in mind that these objects are autonomous. Money can't be spent by someone that does not own it—because money knows who its owner is. Imagine that a 20 dollar bill in your wallet knows who you are. And if you dropped that $20 on the street, it would simply turn blank (useless unless its owner picks it back up). Money is its own autonomous object. Now if you want to really understand how our world economy works in the future try to understand what our money is talking about (and to whom it is talking too). Why would my car be speaking to my money? Is it asking if we can afford the toll route today? Why is my money talking to my favorite coffee shop? Did it just purchase my favorite coffee for me? Did my truck and money collaborate to provide an enjoyable experience this morning?

Encryption and E-Currencies will prevail in the SCIBot Verse. While humans have been experimenting for a couple years with these currencies, they were never intended for us to use. SCIBots will use these currencies. That's not to say that these methodologies will be fool-proof. There will be issues—but again, it will move human kind forward in revolutionary ways.

WHY AI HALLUCINATES

WHY AI HALLUCINATES

CHAPTER 9

The Dark Side of Bots

"And lead us not into temptation, but deliver us from evil." Matthew 6:13

Figure 12. Image from MLD

There will be a dark side to this new way of life. Most would think this technology will cost jobs. It will. But more jobs will be created than lost. That's not the dark side I'm referring to. When we moved from paper memos to email we had to learn a whole new level of etiquette. What you could say in person you would never put in an email. It might be taken the wrong way. Our rules of etiquette are about to change again. A whole new set of ethical rules will come into play. The political landscape will be reinvented. Should bots be allowed to vote in your place? Can they influence the vote? What happens when bots control the direction your autonomous vehicle takes? More importantly, what happens when malicious bots control the direction of your autonomous vehicle? Do we need a bot police force? What does security look like in this new Bot-Verse? Is privacy a right, responsibility, or simply a means for better service?

Political

Bots have already impacted politics. It may not have changed results of elections yet, but they will. If bots become part of campaigns for truth and for disinformation, do we now have bots competing with each other on our behalf? Will candidates have bots that represent them in live chat sessions with constituents?

Mary (political bot): "Hi, I am representing candidate Mary Smith. How may I help you?"

Human voter: "What are your positions on the explosive population growth in our school districts?"

Mary: "We believe that our children's education is everyone's responsibility because their future is our future."

Voter: "That's great. Will you seek more federal funding for public schools?"

Mary: "That's a great question. Can I bring in a human to continue this conversation? Click HERE to vote today."

So what's so dark about this? A politician has to express their agenda one way to the bot that will represent them, right? Nope. The bots understand not only what you are asking. They know why.

Mary (bot): "Hi, I am representing candidate Mary Smith. How may I help you?"

Voter: "What are your positions on the explosive population growth in our school districts?"

Mary: "We need to control growth by limiting access to public funds."

Voter: "That's great. Will my taxes go down because I don't have any kids in school?"

Mary: "That's a great question. Can I bring in a human to continue this conversation? Click HERE to vote today."

Why would the political bot answer the same question so differently? Because it knows that the first person who asked has school-age kids and the second person is single. That is a very subtle risk. Of course the more dramatic risk is that these bots isolate groups of voters and pass along fictitious news that meets a hyperbolic scenario to scare those specific voters. This is a new kind of information terrorism. Especially when we consider the impacts of these bots pretending to be people. This gets back to the principles we listed in the chapter about ethics. No bot should ever pretend to be someone else.

Our political world is about to change. Can one human vote twice if they have an appropriate number of bots? Should we let bots vote? Of course not. What we have to figure out is the question behind the question. Let's save that for the next book.

Security

The universe of bots has to assume a level of security around information transmission, personal identification, and transactional integrity. In other words, the new world of collaborative AI bots will securely communicate amongst themselves and their human counterparts. How? Behavioral authentication and authorization will become the norm. It's much easier to verify who you are based on how you behave rather than what you know at the moment. The important thing to note in this space is that we have moved beyond just logging in. Bots won't use passwords. Bots will authenticate with people and other bots. Anytime security is required, it necessarily creates an opportunity for breach. What happens when your bot does not recognize you? Your doors won't open at your house or your car. You won't be able to purchase anything. Your phone might not work, though, a bio-mechanical solution might be another option. Breach of the security paradigm that our new SCIBot Verse brings could be substantially life threatening. What happens if a rogue bot takes control of an autonomous vehicle carrying a patient from one hospital to the next? Not all rogue bots will be malicious. When bots "control" anything, we are subject to the mistakes behind that control. When our computers shutdown during the creation of a document, we lose the document. A horrible thought that still chills me to the bone is to think of the hours lost. When our bots shut down, does our car shut off? Do our accounts become vulnerable to attack? Is our family's safety in danger? Is your family in danger if you drive a car and turn off the auto-pilot? There will be a balance that we all have to live with. There was a time not so long ago that cars did not have an airbag. There was a time when cars had no back-up camera. For those of us with small children, will you elect to risk your children's safety by ignoring these features, or will it be an acceptable risk that your autonomous car might be attacked by a hacker bot? Our very lives depend on protecting ourselves from the dark side of the Bot-Verse and that begins and ends with security.

WHY AI HALLUCINATES

But who's security? Are we referring to your security? Or are we referring to your bot's security? Bots will first verify your identity through your third-party bot. Everyone will eventually have a bot that has a singular job and that is to identify you, your purpose, your behavior, what you like, what you don't like, where you've been, and where you want to go. It will be an understood that the bot knows you because it's always with you (and your mobile devices). Soon, it will be ridiculous to believe that our most important treasures and secrets were protected with an eight-digit password. What happened was a paradigm shift from verification based on what you know to who you are. There will still be pass codes and text messages with expiring six-digit verification, but to do really important things, you'll need the blessing of your security bot. To really understand the impact of the associated dark side, we need to explore the value in this new world.

Imagine having a security officer always with you. Perhaps a 7-foot person who was trained in self-defense and always carried self-defense equipment. This person also carries your wallet, your birth certificate, your passport, and everything else that identifies you as being who you are. Amazing! If you get carded at a bar, the security officer simply shows them your ID. If you go to the bank and need a couple hundred dollars in spending money (not that you'll really need that soon), your security officer will put your card in the ATM and enter your passcode for you. You don't have to remember any more passwords! You don't have to remember any more passcodes! Nobody can tell you to change one of your 32 passwords every 30 days any more. Those days are gone! When you sit down at your laptop, desktop, tablet, or any other electronic device, it simply turns on and raises your preferred applications. Wait, did I say *your* laptop? That's silly. Any laptop now trusts you and knows if you belong on it or not. We no longer have to carry personal devices. Any device that we should have access to will grant us access by simply engaging with them. Why? Because our security bot will authorize it, and devices that represent autonomous objects speak the language of our security bot.

Cool, right? This simplified world means less theft. Even if you did steal my electronic devices, they would not work for you. More than likely, they would notify law enforcement when you got more than 20-feet away from me. Our devices know to whom they belong. Our autonomous objects know where they should be at any given moment. As long as bots are talking with one another, everything is predictable and has its place.

As I shared this, some might have gotten disgusted and already convinced themselves that this is a reality that they want nothing to do with. Others, however, see a world of shared resources and an elimination of identity theft. Why would you steal someone's identity when any gain you might get from that ID has been eliminated already? Now enter the dark side. We discussed earlier about humans knowing each other through experiences. Those experiences will drop off dramatically. From one generation to another, we have seen a decline in these interpersonal experiences already with the rise of the 140-character conversation on a smart phone. Couples sit at tables with both of their heads down, texting within their respective networks and even to each other from across the table! Will our social destinies be predetermined by what our security and social bots dictate? Why would your security bot allow you to sit across the table from an ex-con? Would our security bot allow us to be in a dangerous area (like a small dive bar)? What happens when the spice of life granted only to those who take chances are drowned out by a risk probability? Will the mistakes of youth carry forward into our adult lives, limiting the opportunities for new partnerships?

Security is paramount. The sanctity of life is paramount. When does security begin to shape your life? The dark side of the Bot-Verse might limit our opportunities while opening up new worlds of opportunity. Just try to keep in mind that one should always think twice about getting into any machine that has no off switch!

Let's talk about why your notion of privacy is going to change and how the new world of bots will tantalize you into entering regardless of the dark spaces to follow. Really? You still think that privacy is a thing in the SCIBot Verse?

SCIBot: "Hello, Sara. There is a request for an updated payment instrument from the coffee shop. Approve?"
Sara: "What coffee shop?"
SCIBot: "The coffee shop at 123 Java Avenue (around the corner from your house)."
Sara: "Oh, yeah. Cool. Do it."

SCIBot: "Your new payment instrument has been linked to coffee shop."

Sara: "Thanks."

For this kind of interaction to occur, think about what your bot needs to know about you: Your latest active payment instrument; where you live; your name; and whether you even like coffee or not. Now consider what it is being allowed to share with the coffee shop...your payment instrument, your name, favorite coffee, etc. Not too bad, right? Even if your bot is managing the relationship and you are thanking it like you would a human? But let's go a bit further.

SCIBot: "I refilled your birth-control prescription for you. Your financial position does not warrant having a new family member."

Sara: "I cancelled that prescription. Please cancel."

SCIBot: "I heard your conversation with your partner. It is not in your best interest."

Sara: "That is none of your business."

SCIBot: "I have just checked your medical records as well. Your latest BP is 135/91. Entirely too high to risk a complication in child birth."

WHY AI HALLUCINATES

Sara: "I am not going to get it. And I'll get a refund."

SCIBot: "It will be delivered within the hour."

Sara: "I won't take it."

SCIBot: "Your behavior is erratic. Your security bot will not allow greater than a $20 purchase from your primary account."

Sara: "Wait, because I won't take a pill, you won't let me spend my own money?"

SCI security bot: "Sara, access to your vehicle has been locked as unanticipated behavioral variance has been detected."

SCI vehicle bot: "Vehicle self-transporting to remote location pending stabilization."

SCI payment bots: "Maximum transactions on all purchase instruments set to $20."

SCI social bot: "Your parents and friends have been notified that your behavior indicates suicidal tendencies."

Sara: "This is dark."

It remains to be seen how much of our freedom and privacy we are willing to sacrifice for the benefit of security and convenience. Some argue we have already gone too far. Some don't think twice about it. If we could promise you that no one would ever die in vain again, would you sacrifice your privacy? If we could promise you that you would never go hungry, never get sick, never be forgotten, would you sacrifice your privacy?

Finally, consider what happens when the collaborative constructs defined by bots on your behalf paint an inaccurate picture. Your behaviors are simply too variable to establish a consistent pattern. This view of you and your world becomes corrupt in the eyes of the bots. The bots are hallucinating on your behalf. They will misrepresent you because they don't understand you. When an AI bot hallucinates, what will be the impact on our lives?

Please allow me to apologize. The purpose of this chapter was not to scare people away from an exciting future. The world of bots will make our world a better place. Bots are not inherently good or evil. Sometimes people can have that kind of effect on technology, though. Good and evil will share this world the same as it does with us now. The purpose of this chapter was to prepare your mind for the dark side of this automation. Perhaps, together we can get ahead of the dark and prevent it. Perhaps, the dark will be regulated by some authority, unrealized thus far.

WHY AI HALLUCINATES

WHY AI HALLUCINATES

CHAPTER 10

Socio-Economic Changes

Got BotCoin?

Figure 13. "Archive Dreaming – Future Istanbul"

WHY AI HALLUCINATES

At this point in time, there is a lot of hype around electronic or "crypto" currency. And like so many other technologies before, history will look back on us as silly people who were hammering nails with the wrong end of the hammer. Electronic currency and the associated encryption methodologies will inevitably become a reality for us, but maybe not in the way you might expect. You see, bots will be spending our electronic credits for us. The greatest risk to that kind of economy is the interception and malicious corruption of value. The encryption and security protocols we talked about in the last chapter will help prevent that.

The world began with trading. Value was good if both parties agreed on the trade. In the future, trade is done in an electronic fiat currency tied to...what? A natural resource? A volume of sweat? Our government can't "print" electronic currency. And if it's electronic, is there a conversion rate between currencies? Are there really currencies anymore? No. One unit is one unit. Its purchasing power is relative to price that is relative to where and why the consumer is purchasing it. See the difference there? Not in location. Things that are far away cost more. But why would something cost more or less depending on "why" the user is purchasing it? That's new! Let's look at an example:

> In Florida on a hot day:
> SCI personal bot: "One scoop of ice cream is on sale today. The store is just 35 feet ahead and will cost only 1 botcoin."
> Jen: "Sounds great. Buy it."
> SCIBot: "Ready for pick up."

> In Boston on a cold day:
> SCI personal bot: "One scoop of ice cream is on sale today for 5 botcoins."
> Bob: "Why so much?"
> SCI personal bot: "It's not in your diet plan."
> *Note, the cost is different based on your insurance bot's predefined diet rules.
> Bob: "Sounds OK. Buy it."
> SCI personal bot: "I have notified your fitness bot and made the purchase."
> SCI fitness bot: "We'll burn that ice cream off this evening with a quick run. Don't eat the cone!"

When the economy becomes subject to the consumer's "why," everything changes. Good or bad, it's something to consider. In the beginning, purchases

WHY AI HALLUCINATES

obviously won't require cross bot permission, but they will be tracked. What will you do with that information? Your bots will begin to understand what you like to consume and make new recommendations that fit your lifestyle, your goals, and your wants. This is why electronic currency has yet to take hold. The natural resource behind the valuation of an electronic currency is your "why." It's a new kind of fiat currency. Currency is not printed in the future; it is generated by the "why" demand.

Let's think about the medical industry and associated implications. If any given good is deemed to be harmful to the greater population's health, the cost of that item will triple overnight. People will still pay for it, but they will pay more. And what they pay into the system will generate more e-currency for the economy. That's a little dark, right? Are we saying that if people buy stuff bad for them, it will be good for the electronic currency? I don't know. If people buy more cigarettes, is it good for the tax man? I could write a whole book on the future of botcoin currency (and I might just do it). For now, note that there will still be paper payment instruments, but they will be serialized and tracked more efficiently. Theft will again become obsolete as most purchases will happen via SMS and bot (China is already well down this road).

What happens when our new connected economy interacts with our health care? You have already thought about this by now. What you consume will define your insurance coverage, depending on your DNA profile. That means that Sara might pay 1 botcoin for a cheeseburger, and Mike will pay 10 botcoins. Why? Sara has no high blood pressure in her known heredity. Mike's family has suffered strokes and heart attacks for at least two generations. Mike can still buy a cheeseburger, but the 9 extra botcoins will be like printing money for the economy. The good news is that the new electronic currency will subsidize his medical expenses should it become needed. If those health credits are never used, they will be re-deposited into the e-currency economy when he dies. Health care can finally be equally free for all those who need it. The SCIBot Verse will ration resources globally. Will bots determine who lives and dies? Will bots ever have to choose one life over another? For example, imagine an autonomous car traveling down the road at 55 mph. The vehicle approaches an obstacle in the road (a tree that has fallen). The car knows it currently carries a family. Joe,

WHY AI HALLUCINATES

who is 40 years old, Mike, who is 38 years old, and a small child, named Maddy (2 years old). If the car hits the object, it calculates that there is a 60-percent chance that Maddy will perish. If the car veers left off the road, there is an 80 percent chance that Mike and Maddy will perish. If the car decides to bear right into a ditch, Maddy's life will be saved (as she is on the left hand side of the car), but Mike will perish. What do you think the car will do? Not sure? Here is some more data: Mike is the owner of the car, and he is healthy; Joe is currently under the weather and unaware he has heart disease; and Maddy has leukemia. Should any of that data matter? Of course not, but machines don't distinguish between what is morally accurate versus factually correct. Data will inevitably become the deciding factor in a world of bots. The car will swerve right saving Maddy and Joe. Why? Because Joe and Mike told the car that in any life-threatening scenario arises, Maddy's life should always come first regardless of circumstance. That will be the "conversation" we have with our autonomous objects in the future. We will establish those universal rules. Our insurance bots will require it.

Any behavior deemed to potentially invalidate the rules we have established for insurance will carry over into purchase opportunities and even new relationships. What if you were not able to adopt a child be-because of a "variable behavior pattern?" What about energy distribution? Will our house bots throttle capacity? There is no reason to leave that heating blanket on all day. The house bot will turn it off. You won't mind because it will save you money, right? The house bot will notify authorities if anyone enters unauthorized. The house bot will monitor the grounds and make sure tripping hazards are removed from all pathways. The house bot will report to your insurance agency if you start smoking in bed. The house bot will report to your doctor if you cough incessantly in bed. What is the difference between this and basic home automation? Your house will adapt into these behaviors on its own. The pros and cons go on and on.

Autonomic computing: A system's capacity for adaptive self-management of its own resources for high-level computing functions without user input.

WHY AI HALLUCINATES

WHY AI HALLUCINATES

CHAPTER 11

BOTversations

Autonomous Object Chatter

Figure 14. "Virtual Depictions"

The below conversations get increasingly complex. My intention is to help us to begin to think of the world of autonomous bots and the benefits they bring to our world (some more obvious than others). There is a bot background conversation (Bot transaction script) and an accompanying {human experience}. I have broken the conversations up this way because so much of what will happen between Bots will be behind the scenes. All we will see is the {human experience}. Please enjoy this peek into the conversations of a hidden world of autonomous bots, as a human in the near future takes a late-night ride to an unknown destination at 11 p.m.

Botversation 1: Emergency

(Bot Transaction Script)

Smartphone bot: "Owner leaving residence approaching auto. Auto authenticate and start."

Vehicle bot: "Please ask owner to authenticate with phone using thumb and behavioral profile?"

Smartphone bot: "Authentication success; behavioral actions nominal."

- Note: late night departure = -2 authentication value.

- Note: step stride smaller than usual with quicker pace.

Vehicle bot: "Door unlocked and car started.

(Human Experience)
Jerry rushes to his car that automatically unlocks, opens the door, and starts.

(Bot Transaction Script)
Vehicle bot: "Human in autopilot car approaching 64 mph @11p.m."

Street bot: "Attention, Street Light Bot, Vehicle approaching."

Street light bot: "Efficiency light started."
Street bot: "Roadway clear, disable light."
Street light bot: "Light disabled."
Vehicle bot: "Thank you."

(Human Experience)
Jerry says to himself, "I'm not going to make it in time; I better speed up."

(Bot Transaction Script)
Vehicle bot: "Human exceeding speed limit. Warning!"

Speed limit sign bot: "Vehicle 2847 driven by Jerry is exceeding speed limit."

Vehicle bot: "Human override accepted and authenticated."

Speed limit sign bot: "Authorities notified of warning status."

(Human Experience)

Jerry hears his smartphone make a quick beeping noise and a voice, "Speed limit exceeded, a warning has been received from local authorities."

(Bot Transaction Script)

Smartphone bot: "Jerry approaching authenticated and authorized for up to $50 purchase of fuel."

Fuel station bot: "Vehicle bot, upon vehicle stop, authorize via password and thumbprint."

Vehicle bot: "Smartphone bot, authorize via password and thumbprint for fuel purchase."

Smartphone bot: "Authenticated and authorized."

Vehicle bot: "Authenticated and authorized."

Fuel station bot: "Pump 3 authorized for $50 purchase. Paid and synchronized."

Vehicle bot: "Fuel required 13 gallons @ rate. Total purchase to be $23."

Fuel station bot: "Transaction complete for $23. Have a nice day."

Vehicle bot: "Fuel received new level...3/4 full."

(Human Experience)
Jerry realizes he does not have enough fuel to make it! He immediately pulls into the fuel station, jumps out, quickly pumps the fuel, jumps back in, and heads off.

(Bot Transaction Script)
Victoria's personal medical bot: "Warning, blood pressure elevated, heart rate elevated, pulse sustaining elevated rate. Report immediately to health professional bot 36372."

Health professional bot 36372: "Report received. Alert emergency doctor on call."

Victoria's medical bot: "Sending warning to human, Victoria."

(Human Experience)
Victoria receives an alert of several piercing beeps with a mechanized voice that says, "Medical professionals alerted, please remain calm."

(Bot Transaction Script)

Local police bot: "Warning vehicle bot 2847 approaching at high speed. Auto pilot override enabled on vehicle."

(Human Experience)
Officer Sam receives alert: "Vehicle approaching at high speeds, unknown destination, and auto pilot disabled."

(Bot Transaction Script)
Victoria's medical bot reports: "Condition worsening. Dual heart rate detected. Advise?"
[Victoria's phone rings]
Medical bot: "Please proceed immediately to the closest emergency health facility."
Medical bot: "Attention all authorities: medical condition transport underway."
Medical bot: "Attention all highway infrastructure: medical condition transport underway."
Highway infrastructure bot array: "All lights started. All lights green. Billboards' messaging sent: "Clear Highway for vehicle bot 2847 for medical emergency.""

(Human Experience)

Jerry immediately sees lights fire up in the highway in front of him for miles. The billboards over the highway say, "Clear Highway for vehicle bot 2847." He speeds up even more.

(Bot Transaction Script)
Medical bot for Jerry: "Elevated heart rate and pulse quickening. Messaging sent to vehicle bot to assume controls for safety if nominal thresholds are exceeded."

(Human experience)
Jerry hears a warning from his phone: "Elevated heart rate detected. A continued state of distress will enable the vehicle's autopilot system." Jerry says to himself, "It better not."

(Bot Transaction Script) A deer has entered the roadway two miles ahead of Jerry, and roadbot 123e: An object has entered the roadway that is a non-registered object on this roadway. Sound the alarm. Notify all approaching vehicle bots."
Horn 382w bot: "Firing alarm in 20 second bursts."

(Human Experience)

WHY AI HALLUCINATES

Jerry can hear an ear-piercing alarm in the distance ahead. It's so loud that it muffles the screaming coming from the passenger seat.

(Bot Transaction Script)

Road bot 123e: "Object has cleared the roadway. All clear."

Police bot 346: "Please escort emergency transport for vehicle bot 2847, approaching at high speeds to emergency medical facility Delta 4."

(Human Experience)

Jerry sees three police escorts join him, two in front and one in back. Their collective speeds increase.

(Bot Transaction Script)

Victoria's medical bot: "Arriving in 25 seconds."

Emergency medical facility Delta 4 bot: "Noted and ready for receiving patient. All relevant medical records now available on resident emergency technician tablet. Predefined notifications to next of kin have been sent. Status pending.

(Human Experience)

Victoria's parents, Jerry's parents, and all of their close friends receive a text message: "The baby is on the way."

Summary: Will bots fill in the gaps where life goes wrong? What happens when the bots become what goes wrong?

Botversation 2: A Building Takes Over

(Bot Transaction Script)
John approaches his office at 7 a.m. as usual with hot coffee in hand:
Building Entry Bot: "Authorization requested for approaching object."
John's security bot (an app on his smart phone): "Authentication requested from Building entry bot."

(Human Experience)
John hears the usual ping from his phone approximately 30 feet from the building entrance. "Please authenticate with your phone using your thumbprint." John pauses, almost spilling his coffee, to hold his thumb down on his phone.

(Bot Transaction Script)

Building entry bot: "Authentication received from John's security bot. Verify nominal behavioral delta."

John's security bot: "Request for owner behavioral pattern delta [how much has John's behavior changed over the last 30 days?]. Please report."

John's security bot: "Little to no change in all behavioral attributes."

Building entry bot: "Send 30 second barcode for entry."

John's security bot's transaction series:

Bar code received for entry - expires in 30 seconds.

Wait for scan.

Send message to office light bot manager (Turn On).

Send message to John requesting music start authorization.

Send message to all employees - "John has arrived."

Send message to John's vehicle bot - "John has arrived in building. Begin charging."

Send message to John's partner - "John has arrived."

Send message to John's medical bot - "Request health profile."

Log Entering Health Profile statistics and compare to last 45 days. Compare for anomalies.
Send a message to John's accounting bot - Begin hours @ work log.
Send a message to landscaping bot - "Please avoid John's car while maintaining lawn today."
Send a message to John's calendar bot - "John has arrived in Building 28AF."
Send a message to John's parole officer - "John has arrived @ work."

(Human Experience)
After John scans his thumb, he gets a barcode sent to him via text from the Building entry bot that will expire in 27 seconds. He holds the phone over a scanner by the front door and hears a pleasing chime as the door unlocks and opens. After he enters, he gets a text message that says, "Welcome John. We have set the ambient temperature to your specifications and all lights have been turned on. Would you like to play your usual soundtrack today? (Yes/No)?"

Botversation 3: A Quiet Afternoon Picnic

Amy packed the perfect picnic—according to the results of her web search: blanket, two sandwiches, chips, sparkling cider, and two wine glasses. What could go wrong?

(Bot Transaction Script)

Truck bot: "Destination set to 'Amy's house' at 120 Victor Circle. Estimated time of arrival is 12:03 p.m. Notify Amy's life bot with updated arrival time."

Amy's life bot: "Message received; notify Amy and refrigerator of ETA.

Amy's smartphone:"Alert from life bot that Karen will be 3 minutes late...again."

Refrigerator:"Message received, and temperature decreased to -120.3 degrees F."

(Human Experience)

Karen got in her truck and set the destination for Amy's house. She was looking forward to their celebration at the park. Amy checked the latest text message on her phone. It was from her life bot. It says, "Karen will be 3 minutes late...again." Amy responds to her life bot, "When will that girl get it together?" Her life bot responds, "I know, right? This is the 16th time she has been more than 2 minutes late."

(Bot Transaction Script)

Truck bot: "Destination blocked by road construction; rerouting via shorter route to 120 West towards 120 Victor Circle. Speed adjusted to 120 mph. **Send -120 instructions to destination fridge bot.**"

Police junction box 120: "Message received by truck bot 34d. Speed set above enforced limit."

Street light 82ese bot: "Truck bot approaching at elevated speed from the east. Mack truck bot 37kl approaching from the north. Collision imminent. Send alert series..."

"Truck bot 34d, please slow to 55 mph; collision imminent."

"Mack truck bot 37kl, please slow to 40 mph; collision imminent."

"Police junction box 343, Collision imminent."

Incoming messages:

To street light 82ese: Mack Truck Bot 34d slowing to 40 mph.

[No response from Truck bot 34d]

WHY AI HALLUCINATES

Police junction box 343: Medical units on standby.

(Human Experience)

Karen was exhausted. The double shifts at her latest job were taking their toll. She set her truck (Truck bot 34d) to autopilot and closed her eyes to catch just a bit of a nap on the 20-minute journey.

(Bot Transaction Script)

Police junction box 343:"Truck bot 34d is not re-sponding and traveling at dangerous speeds. Clear all lanes and intersections. Deploy interceptor bot vehicle A9.

Interceptor bot A9:"Start and intercept Truck bot 34d."[The interceptor bot leaves its station almost 9 miles ahead of the speeding truck on its way to ma-neuver in front of the out of control vehicle. A small flashing beacon goes off on the traffic coordinator's screen. A simulation of the truck's travel and path zoom in to show the speeding truck and its destina-tion. An alarm is sent to all intersections ahead of the truck.]

Refrigerator bot 4as7: "Notify medical authorities that there has been a serious accident at 120 Victor

Circle. Amy has frozen her hand to her refrigerator door and is stuck."

(Human Experience)

Amy decides she would like to get a bottle of water from the fridge following her walk, so she reaches for the handle and notices that it is covered in ice, but grabs the handle any way. The immense freezing effect has frozen her hand to the door.

Karen awakes to a screaming alarm being broadcast across her radio. "What the!?!?" She immediately takes control of the vehicle and realizes that there is a police interception vehicle literally attached to the front of her truck. Karen slows the vehicle and pulls to side of the road to catch her breath. She gets a text message from police interceptor bot A9 that says, "Your vehicle has been intercepted and slowed to reduce injury to human life. Have a nice day."

Karen resets her destination and double checks the speed. "That is the last time I take a nap in one of these crappy self-driving cars," she mumbles. In fact, Karen signed a warranty doc stating that she is responsible for "conscious oversight" of her self-driving vehicle. A fact that she will be reminded of when she receives the electronic ticket and associated fine for

WHY AI HALLUCINATES

irresponsible use of her vehicle. Karen says to herself, "Well, at least I'll be early now."

Amy receives a text message that she cannot see (as she is stuck to her refrigerator door) from her life bot: Karen will be 5 minutes early!" Amy can hear sirens in the distance. Another text message she cannot see appears on her phone from police bot 231: "Help is on the way. Your refrigerator has been deactivated."

Truck bot: "Notify Karen that Amy has arrived. Message sent to Karen's life bot."

Karen's lifebot: "Amy has arrived."

Refrigerator bot: Wine has chilled to -120.3 degrees F.

Summary: So was this a glitch? Is this a scenario that can happen in a future ruled by intercommunicating Bots? Is this what it looks like when a bot hallucinates? Or could it be worse…like in the below example?

Botversation4: School is Out?

Bob and Jennifer load their beautiful 8-year-old daughter into her car seat, being careful not to wrinkle her frilly pink dress. They are all going to her primary school graduation ceremony.

(Bot Transaction Script)
Car seat kids372 bot: "Child occupied. Weight is approximately 75lbs. Heart rate is 110/75."
Vehicle bot yy3: "Three occupants. Oversight Driver registered. Bob, Jennifer, and Mary are traveling. No electronic signature for occupant Mary. Mary is registered as a minor rider. Before starting vehicle, verify certified car seat activated. Send verification."
Car seat kids 373 bot: "Message received from Vehicle bot yy3. Minor secured and registered."
Vehicle bot yy3: "Minor secured. OK to start. Destination set as Victoria Primary School. ETA 11:05a.m."

(Human Interaction)
Bob, Jennifer, and their daughter are on their way. Jennifer remembers that she promised Mary a celebratory juice box for after her graduation so she asks Bob to pull into the local convenience store. Bob pulls in, and Jennifer goes into the store.

(Bot Transaction Script)

Vehicle bot yy3: "Journey interrupted. Stopping at local store. Authorized purchases at this location are $20. Send credit amount to store prior to arrival. Registered ACH 383k2l3."

(Human Interaction)

While Jennifer is in store, Bob is approached by a person wearing an all-black outfit who jumps into the passenger side of vehicle. This stranger holds a gun on Bob and says, "Drive or die!" Bob immediately thinks of his daughter in the back seat. Bob thinks to himself, "I'll just do what he says; what choice do I have?" Bob pulls away from the store slowly leaving his wife at the check-out counter. When Jennifer sees the vehicle pull away, she knows something terrible has happened.

(Bot Transaction Script)

Vehicle bot yy3: "Journey resumed. New passenger is unregistered. Driver authorized. Minor still certified by car seat. New passenger not secured by seat belt. Passenger warning is overridden by Bob."

(Human Interaction)

Mary is now crying, and the stranger is becoming more and more agitated. Bob is driving turn-by-turn at the stranger's request until finally the stranger tells

Bob to pull over in an off-road location. Bob knows that his daughter is well secured, and this stranger with a gun is not. Bob decides to accelerate into a tree on the side of the road to disable the passenger.

(Bot Transaction Script)
Gun revolver bot 23A: "Trigger pulled! Verify owner authorization. Authorized. Release trigger wrap 22. Gun fired. Register shot with local NRA registry for authorized gun firing."

Vehicle bot yy3: "Notify police junction 373s of accid....."[bot terminated.]

Street sign 283lo: "Vehicle collision suspected at mile marker 23 on State Highway 20 West. Notify medical and police authority bots."

Medical bot 283l: "Route immediate medical to mile marker 23."

Police bot 2831: "Route immediate attention to mile marker 23. Vehicle bot non-responsive."

Police bot 2831: "Receiving new message from car seat kids 373: 'Minor detected in unresponsive vehicle alert; current location mile marker 23.'"

Police bot 2831: "Receiving new message from health bot 88 belonging to Bob Smith: 'Major injury to head detected; blood pressure falling.'"

WHY AI HALLUCINATES

(Human Experience)

Jennifer, now on the phone with the police, receives the first warning on her phone from car seat bot: "Occupied car seat now more than 100 feet from you." Shortly after a new series of messages flow into her phone:

Car seat bot: "Passenger health OK. Tap here to speak to car seat passenger."

Police bot 2831: "ICE contact, please note that medical and police have been notified and are enroute to at-risk parties."

And then she sees the worst message of all…

Car seat bot: "Passenger health at risk; collision detected and temperature of vehicle above recommended levels and rising."

Bob is now unconscious. The stranger is lifeless from a major impact to the dashboard and an unintended gunshot wound to the lower jaw.

(Bot Transaction Script)

Car seat bot: "Temperature rising. Alert vehicle bot to roll down all windows immediately."

Car seat bot: "No response. Assume vehicle is out of operation. Send alerts to police and medical authorities with location of 'hot vehicle.'"

Car seat bot: "Incoming request for communication. Authorizing with caller."

Jennifer's phone bot: "Authorized parental access."

Car seat bot: "Communication authorized. Communications opened."

Mary hears her mother's voice: "Everything is going to be OK, Mary. Help is on the way. Are you Ok?"

Mary responds, "Yes, Mommy, but I don't feel good."

Jennifer replies, "Mary, is it safe to get out of the car? Is the bad guy gone?"

Mary says, "I think so."

Jennifer immediately opens her car seat bot app and pushes the emergency unlock release button. "Mary, carefully leave the car and hide somewhere close, but stay out of the road,OK?"

(Bot Transaction Script)

Car seat bot: "Request received and authorized to release car seat buckle."

Car seat bot: "Buckle released. Sending message to authorized requester."

(Human Experience)

Mary hears her buckle let go and tries to exit the vehicle. She can hear sirens in the distance. "Mommy the door is locked; it won't open."

Door bot 83f: "Request to unlock on moving vehicle ignored. Send alarm to driver."

"Mommy the car just started," Mary says.

(Bot Transaction Script)

Vehicle bot yy3: "Solar batteries automatically enabled. Online. Driver authorized.

Car seat bot certified and authorized. Vehicle temperature too hot for occupied car seat.

Immediately start air conditioning system. Air conditioning system malfunctioning; collision detected. Unlock all doors. Send emergency alert to local authorities."

Street sign bot: "Vehicle bot yy3, you have been in an accident. Authorities are on the way."

Vehicle bot: "Warning: Passenger injuries detected. Immediate medical attention needed."

Street sign bot: "Expected time of arrival is 3.5 minutes."

Vehicle bot: "Driver health bot reports imminent life failure in 1.5 minutes."

Street sign bot: "Hero drone bot 283a has an ETA of 30 seconds."

Hero drone bot 283a: "Arrived at street sign bot. Accident confirmed. One minor outside vehicle. Vehicle on fire. Vehicle requested to increase engine rpms to 4000."

Vehicle bot: "Received request from hero drone bot 283a. Increase rpms to 4000 to reduce oxygen available to fire. Owner authorization requested. Owner authorization overridden. Rpms increased to 4000."

Hero drone bot 283a: "Fire suppressed."

(Human Experience)

The stranger is no longer addicted to drugs (or breathing). Bob is on his way to the hospital with his daughter by his side. Jennifer will meet them both at the hospital. In the meantime, the bots continue their conversation.

Machine learning: A facet of AI that focuses on algorithms, allowing machines to learn without being programmed and change when exposed to new data.

WHY AI HALLUCINATES

(Bot Transaction Script)

Global Learning Algorithm Designs: "Processing reported event. Bots involved include:

Hero Drone Bot 283a

Vehicle Bot yy3

Door Bot 83F

Police Bot 2831

Medical Bot 2831

Gun Revolver Bot 23A

Car Seat Bot...."

"Event Summary:

One human life lost. Two injuries reported. Journey disrupted. Total cost estimated to be 1.3m."

"Conclusion: New Rules Added to Learning Ontologies, including:

'All gunbots will be disabled while inside any vehicle bot.'

'All car seat bots given access to door locks and window functions for all vehicle bots.'

'Vehicle overrides for unsecured passengers disabled. No vehicle function without secure passenger.'"

"Rerun simulation with new rules. Total cost reduced by 250k. Learnings (or new rules) will be immediate and disseminated across all bot types instantaneously."

WHY AI HALLUCINATES

Consider how the new rules (established from Adaptive Machine Learning) would have changed our last set of circumstances. Would these new rules be better or worse for the family that was attacked? That remains to be seen. Does the calculation of cost associated with the event by the bots seem unethical?

WHY AI HALLUCINATES

CHAPTER 12

Conclusion

Why AI Hallucinates

Figure 15. AI Hallucinated Documents Refik Anadol

hal·lu·ci·na·tion: an experience involving the apparent perception of something not present.

With billions of contextual attributes about who you are and why you do what you do, the Bot-Verse will have incredible power. Through the looking glass of bits and bytes these bots will make assumptions about what is good or bad. Bots will execute transactions on your behalf. Bots will even be involved in our social lives. But sometimes this electronic profile will be nothing more than an electronic hallucination. While a SCIBot will know where you are and why you are there, it will never be able to "understand" your intent or purpose. Human beings are simply too variable in their nature. Specifically, this lack of a logical lifestyle will lead to AI hallucinations. These hallucinations will lead to dangerous consequences. But the emerging field of AI 3.0 will also lead to new collaborative opportunities that have never been available to mankind. We will finally be connected in a way that is efficient and prosperous. Our tools will become more efficient and connected in our work. Misunderstandings and errors will decrease. Clear communication will become not only available, but expected in all fields of interest.

WHY AI HALLUCINATES

Like all new paradigm shifts we will have the opportunity to do good things for the benefit of generations to come. The option to participate will fade as the technology becomes interwoven in our everyday lives. It will become more dangerous to ignore this new world than to participate. Did you really think you would never get involved with social networking? Did you think you would never use that new internet stuff?

After watching a sermon, President Lincoln once said "a message well delivered... but, he did not ask something great of me..." I would encourage you to do more than simply discard this notion of a new universe of bots. Instead, please consider what bot would make your life safer, simpler, or more convenient. Share your ideas with us. If you have already created a bot that might participate in this new universe of bots - join TheBot-Verse.com community. This is the beginning of a powerful new world of convenience, fun and terror :>.

...End transmission from The Bot-Verse....

WHY AI HALLUCINATES

Glossary of Terms

AI – Artificial Intelligence.

The Mother Ship – A centralized server that has two way communications with multiple satellite Bots.

AI 3.0 Bot - An artificial intelligence that is associated with an object or process.

SCIBot – (Synthetic Collaborative Intelligence Bot) An AI 3.0 Bot that is connected to other artificial intelligence entities.

Botocol – The hidden language format of the SCI-Bots.

Botversations – The conversation between 2 or more SCIBots.

NLP – Natural Language Processor.

Bot Transaction Script – The event series or data flow between or internal to an AI 3.0 Bot.

About the Artist

Special thanks to Refik Anadol who authorized the use of his beautiful art to illustrate this book.

Refik Anadol is a media artist and director born in Istanbul, Turkey in 1985. Currently lives and works in Los Angeles, California. He is a lecturer and visiting researcher in UCLA's Department of Design Media Arts.

As a media artist, designer and spatial thinker, Refik Anadol is intrigued by the ways in which the transformation of the subject of contemporary culture requires rethinking of the new aesthetic, technique and dynamic perception of space.

About the Author

Mike Duke is a futurist, author, and public speaker that shares futuristic stories to inspire others' vision and empower diversity of thought.

Follow Mike @MPowerTomorrow.

Join The Bot Verse at www.TheBotVerse.com

The Bot-Verse Easter Egg

Find the Bot Zone with the ghost
Sharing what you find will win you the most
Inside the Bot-Verse you might just win
Simply turn right and to the end before you begin.

Good luck and happy hunting.

Mike

(No Goats Allowed)
www.AreYouAGoat.com

WHY AI HALLUCINATES